Baird

by Murray Ogilvie

LangSyne
PUBLISHING
WRITING *to* REMEMBER

LangSyne

PUBLISHING

WRITING *to* REMEMBER

Vineyard Business Centre,
Pathhead, Midlothian EH37 5XP
Tel: 01875 321 203 Fax: 01875 321 233
E-mail: info@lang-syne.co.uk
www.langsyneshop.co.uk

Design by Dorothy Meikle
Printed by Ricoh Print Scotland
© Lang Syne Publishers Ltd 2011

ISBN 978-1-85217-286-2

Baird

RELATED NAMES:

Baard
Bard
Barde
Beard
Beird
MacBard

Baird

MOTTO:
Dominus fecit
- "The Lord made".

CREST:
An Eagle's Head.

TERRITORY:
Peebleshire and Lanarkshire.

Chapter one:

The origins of the clan system

by Rennie McOwan

The original Scottish clans of the Highlands and the great families of the Lowlands and Borders were gatherings of families, relatives, allies and neighbours for mutual protection against rivals or invaders.

Scotland experienced invasion from the Vikings, the Romans and English armies from the south. The Norman invasion of what is now England also had an influence on land-holding in Scotland. Some of these invaders stayed on and in time became 'Scottish'.

The word clan derives from the Gaelic language term 'clann', meaning children, and it was first used many centuries ago as communities were formed around tribal lands in glens and mountain fastnesses.

The format of clans changed over the centuries, but at its best the chief and his family held the land on behalf of all, like trustees, and the ordinary clansmen and women believed they had a blood relationship with the founder of their clan.

There were two way duties and obligations. An inadequate chief could be deposed and replaced by someone of greater ability.

Clan people had an immense pride in race. Their relationship with the chief was like adult children to a father and they had a real dignity.

The concept of clanship is very old and a more feudal notion of authority gradually crept in.

Pictland, for instance, was divided into seven principalities ruled by feudal leaders who were the strongest and most charismatic leaders of their particular groups.

By the sixth century the 'British' kingdoms of Strathclyde, Lothian and Celtic Dalriada (Argyll) had emerged and Scotland, as one nation, began to take shape in the time of King Kenneth MacAlpin.

Some chiefs claimed descent from

ancient kings which may not have been accurate in every case.

By the twelfth and thirteenth centuries the clans and families were more strongly brought under the central control of Scottish monarchs.

Lands were awarded and administered more and more under royal favour, yet the power of the area clan chiefs was still very great.

The long wars to ensure Scotland's independence against the expansionist ideas of English monarchs extended the influence of some clans and reduced the lands of others.

Those who supported Scotland's greatest king, Robert the Bruce, were awarded the territories of the families who had opposed his claim to the Scottish throne.

In the Scottish Borders country - the notorious Debatable Lands - the great families built up a ferocious reputation for providing warlike men accustomed to raiding into England and occasionally fighting one another.

Chiefs had the power to dispense justice

and to confiscate lands and clan warfare produced a society where martial virtues - courage, hardiness, tenacity - were greatly admired.

Gradually the relationship between the clans and the Crown became strained as Scottish monarchs became more orientated to life in the Lowlands and, on occasion, towards England.

The Highland clans spoke a different language, Gaelic, whereas the language of Lowland Scotland and the court was Scots and in more modern times, English.

Highlanders dressed differently, had different customs, and their wild mountain land sometimes seemed almost foreign to people living in the Lowlands.

It must be emphasised that Gaelic culture was very rich and story-telling, poetry, piping, the clarsach (harp) and other music all flourished and were greatly respected.

Highland culture was different from other parts of Scotland but it was not inferior or less sophisticated.

Central Government, whether in London

*"The spirit of the clan means much
to thousands of people"*

or Edinburgh, sometimes saw the Gaelic clans as a challenge to their authority and some sent expeditions into the Highlands and west to crush the power of the Lords of the Isles.

Nevertheless, when the eighteenth century Jacobite Risings came along the cause of the Stuarts was mainly supported by Highland clans.

The word Jacobite comes from the Latin for James - Jacobus. The Jacobites wanted to restore the exiled Stuarts to the throne of Britain.

The monarchies of Scotland and England became one in 1603 when King James VI of Scotland (1st of England) gained the English throne after Queen Elizabeth died.

The Union of Parliaments of Scotland and England, the Treaty of Union, took place in 1707.

Some Highland clans, of course, and Lowland families opposed the Jacobites and supported the incoming Hanoverians.

After the Jacobite cause finally went down at Culloden in 1746 a kind of ethnic cleansing took place. The power of the chiefs was curtailed. Tartan and the pipes were banned in law.

Many emigrated, some because they wanted to, some because they were evicted by force. In addition, many Highlanders left for the cities of the south to seek work.

Many of the clan lands became home to sheep and deer shooting estates.

But the warlike traditions of the clans and the great Lowland and Border families lived on, with their descendants fighting bravely for freedom in two world wars.

Remember the men from whence you came, says the Gaelic proverb, and to that could be added the role of many heroic women.

The spirit of the clan, of having roots, whether Highland or Lowland, means much to thousands of people.

*Clan warfare produced a society where
courage and tenacity were greatly admired.*

Chapter two:

Patriots and radicals

Over the centuries the Baird clan has given the world men who were patriots and traitors, lawmakers and lawbreakers, entrepreneurs and radicals, an accomplished scholar and a great general. The clan has descended from an ancient family whose Scottish roots are in modern-day Peebleshire and Lanarkshire. From humble beginnings they spread their influence at home and abroad in many fields leaving the world with a lasting legacy.

According to legend the Bairds first came to prominence during the time of William I, known as William the Lion, the king of Scots who reigned from 1165 to 1214. William is credited with founding Arbroath Abbey, the site of the later Declaration of Arbroath. However, he is best known for adopting the use of the Lion Rampant on his flag. It was a red lion on a yellow background which is still in use today.

The king was on a hunting expedition in southwest Scotland when he became separated from his retinue. There are two versions of what happened next. The first and most common is that he was attacked by a wild boar and a man named Baird, who'd accompanied the king in the hunting party, leapt to the monarch's defence and slayed the boar. The other version is that the king was attacked by a wild bear! There were records of bears in Britain at around that time, but they were culled by royal decree and none survived.

Whatever happened, Mr Baird was given large areas of land by a grateful king. In those days they spelt their name Bard or Barde. Baird did not come in to common usage until the 16th century. These earlier versions of the name reflect the belief that the family had emigrated to England from southern France during the reign of William of Normandy, known as William the Conqueror, who invaded England in 1066. There is a record of a French-sounding Henry de Barde witnessing the granting of a charter of lands in Stirling to the Bishop of Glasgow by King William in 1178.

In the reign of Alexander III of Scotland (1241-1286) Richard Baird received the lands of Meikle and Little Kyp in Lanarkshire, which are probably situated near the modern day Strathaven and Lesmahagow.

By the late 13th century the Bairds had become prosperous and highly-respected. So much so they were signatories to the Ragman Roll. This was a record of the acts of fealty and homage which King Edward I of England forced Scotland's nobility and gentry to sign in 1292.

Edward was known as The Hammer of the Scots because of his attempts to impose his rule on the land north of the border. Initially, Edward had planned to annex Scotland through marriage. His intention was for his son and heir Edward to marry Margaret the Maid of Norway. She was the daughter of King Eirik II of Norway and Margaret, daughter of King Alexander III of Scotland. The princess was born in 1283 and was sometimes known as Margaret of Scotland and was considered to have been Queen of Scots from 1286 until she died in 1290 with no successor.

There were fears that without a clear-cut heir to the Scottish throne a power vacuum would develop and the country would descend into tribal war. In order to prevent this Edward was invited by the nobility and other power brokers of the time to rule on who would be the next king. In return he insisted on the signatures to the Ragman Roll. In November 1292, in the castle at Berwick-upon-Tweed, Edward chose John Balliol.

Among the signatories were Fergus de Baird, of Meikle and Little Kyp, who records suggest headed a large and wealthy family. With him were John Baird, of Evandale, and Robert Baird of Cambusnethan.

In 1296, however, Edward invaded Scotland. The Scottish resistance was led by Sir William Wallace. Wallace fought a courageous running battle against the English until his capture in 1305. Jordan Baird fought alongside him for many years. But not all Bairds of that time were Scots patriots. In 1308 Baird of Carnwath, along with three or four other Bairds were convicted of a conspiracy against King Robert the Bruce and were executed. Their lands in Carnwath were given to Sir Alexander Stuart of Darnley.

While those Bairds were falling foul of the law other family members were in the king's favour. In 1310 the Barony of Cambusnethan, in Lanark, was granted to Robert Baird by Robert the Bruce. At around the same time another Baird was dispensing the law. He was Thomas de Bard of Posso, Sheriff of Peebles. It was his family who eventually spread their wings and moved to the north of Scotland, where they established a dynasty lasting two centuries, which became the main family line.

During the reign of King David II of Scotland (1324-71) the Cambusnethan estate passed from the Bairds through marriage to Sir Alexander Stewart of Darnley and Crookston. Meanwhile the Bairds were on the move. They first settled in Fife, then Banffshire, but eventually they based themselves in Auchmedden, Aberdeenshire, which Andrew Baird bought from the Earl of Buchan in 1539. It was to be their home for more than 200 years.

George Baird of Auchmedden cemented the family's importance locally when, in 1550, he married Elizabeth, the daughter of Alexander Keith of Troop, the brother of the Earl Marischal. This title was first created for the Keith family during the reign of Malcolm IV (1141-1165). The role of the Marischal was to serve as custodian of the Royal Regalia of Scotland and to protect the king when attending parliament. George Baird's descendants became hereditary sheriffs of Aberdeen, and from them came the Bairds of Newbyth and Saughtonhall. Near the end of the 17th century John Baird was created a Baronet with the courtesy title of Lord Newbyth.

Despite his newly-created stature, George Baird soon found himself in trouble with the authorities.

In 1562 he helped his friend the Earl Huntly at the Battle of Corrichie, when the Clan Cameron, supporters of Mary, Queen of Scots, defeated the Earl. Baird tried to spirit his pal away but Huntly died at the scene.

After George's death in 1593 the

Auchmedden Baird line almost came to an end. He left five sons. Andrew emigrated to France where he became a scholar of great note as professor of philosophy and science at the university of Lyon. He later became a monk. Alexander became a businessman trading between the northeast of Scotland and Scandinavia. He left two daughters who were unmarried. Little is known about Patrick except that he lived in the north of Scotland. George was a wine merchant who had two sons. One, Andrew had a son and grandson but after that the line ended. It was left to George's first-born and heir, Gilbert, to ensure the family's longevity. And boy did he oblige. His marriage to the heiress of Ordinhnivas produced 32 sons and daughters.

The Bairds of Auchmeden were also the subject of a curious prophecy. On the estate at Auchmedden a pair of eagles inhabited the nearby rocks of Penan. Thomas the Rhymer predicted, that when the eagles disappeared the estate would pass from the Baird family. Thomas the Rhymer was born near the modern-day Earlston in

Berwickshire. His original name was Thomas
Rimor de Ercildoun. According to a poem he
wrote about himself Thomas saw the Queen of the
Fairies in the Eildon Hills and returned with her to
her kingdom under the hills. When he re-surfaced
he found he had been with the queen for three
years and during that time she had given him the
ability to see into the future. Amongst his suc-
cessful predictions were the death of King
Alexander III in 1286, the defeat of King James
IV at the Battle of Flodden in 1513 and the Union
of the Crowns of Scotland and England in 1603.
One of his other prophesies was "Tide, tide,
whate'er betide, There'll aye be Haigs at
Bemersyde". The Haigs owned the land until
1867 and it looked as though that prediction had
failed. But in 1921 it was bought for Field
Marshall Earl Haig.

What made the Bairds prophesy so mys-
terious is that they moved to Auchmeden in the
middle of the 14th century yet Thomas lived 100
years earlier. So not only did he foresee the eagles
but he must have known the Bairds would end up

in that part of Scotland, so far from their original home. Whatever the connection, legend has it that when the estate was bought by the Earl of Aberdeen, the eagles disappeared. They only returned when Lord Haddo the Earl's heir married Christian Baird, but disappeared again when the estate passed to the Gordons.

Chapter three:

Men of vision and valour

In the early 21st century High Definition TV became all the rage. But any member of the Baird clan could point out that it was old technology. In fact it was around 70 years old. It was first created by a humble, unhealthy minister's son from Helensburgh.

John Logie Baird was the inventor of television. But he was so far ahead of his time that the industry only caught up with his vision in the 1990s, around 65 years later. In addition to TV he was also closely involved in the discovery and implementation of radar and fibre optics. Yet despite his brilliance and years of perseverance he earned almost nothing in return.

Baird was born on August 14, 1888, the son of a Presbyterian minister. Like most young boys he was obsessed by making things. In his case, though, he took matters a bit further and showed early signs of ingenuity by devising a telephone exchange to connect his pals in the street. He also invented an electric lighting system for his home.

Baird attended a local school before going to Glasgow and West of Scotland Technical College (which later became the University of Strathclyde) and Glasgow University to study electrical engineering. His studies were interrupted by the first world war and he never graduated. He moved to Hastings in the south of England where he tested his first 30-line mechanical TV in 1925. He called it the Televisor and it's first public viewing was in at Selfridge's Department Store in London. Amazed viewers saw a flickering image of a doll on a tiny screen.

For much of the time Baird was living on the breadline, relying on financial help from friends and private investors. With their assistance he continued to make breakthroughs. Using post office telephone lines, he sent TV images from London to Glasgow. In 1928 he achieved the world's first transatlantic TV transmission when he sent images to Hartsdale, New York.

However his original technology was overtaken
by electronic television developed by EMI, which
worked on 405 lines of vision. The BBC chose
EMI over Baird when it started broadcasting.

Undeterred, Baird went on to invent sev-
eral other TV-linked creations. They included
phonovision (the forerunner of today's video
recorder), noctovision (an infra-red system for
seeing in the dark), and the first High Definition
color TV. Before he died in 1946, Baird was
working on plans for a television with 1000 lines
of resolution and he had earlier patents for television with up to 1700 lines of resolution. The world
would not catch up with him until 1990 when the
Japanese came up with a TV with 1125 lines of
resolution per frame.

In 1943 Baird asked a government task
force examining the future of television to consid-
er high definition systems of a 1000 lines or more.
The committee agreed with his recommendations.
But he died three years later without seeing his
great vision take shape.

Today, the vast majority of TV programmes are pre-recorded, the system envisaged by Baird as far back as the 1930s. The genius of his technologica advances were not fully recognized until much later when Sony developed the Trinitron Tube, based on his original ideas.

Sir David Baird, a descendant of the Auchmedden family, played a leading role in one of the most famous actions in the history of the British army — the Battle of Perimbancum. In1780, as a captain in the grenadiers of the 73rd regiment, he was posted to India. On arrival he and his untried troops were sent immediately to the aid of a force commanded by Colonel Baillie, which had been pinned down by Hyder Ali. Ali, a shia muslim, and ruler of the Kingdom of Mysore in southern India, went on to become the most formidable military opponent the British faced in the sub-continent.

Baird was part of a 1000-strong detachment under Colonel Fletcher which joined up with Baillie's forces. On September 10, 1780 they marched unwittingly into a carefully prepared ambush set by Ali and his French advisors. Within less than half an hour they were surrounded on all sides facing around 60,000 enemy supported by 60 cannons. Despite these momumental odds Captain Baird kept his cool and kept his own cannons firing. The British, in the form of a square, stood firm, seemingly oblivious to the perils they faced and were described by amazed French officers in Hyder Ali's camp as if acting on a parade ground. After three hours Baird's ten cannons had repulsed onslaught after onslaught. The cream of Ali's army had been obliterated and the losses on his side were massive. The Indians were just about to order the retreat to save the rest of their forces from being slaughtered when terrible misfortune befell the British. The carts which carried their ammunition suddenly exploded in their midst, destroying much of their artillery and leaving a gaping hole in their defences. Hyder's cavalry, led by his son Tippoo, seized the initiative and cut through the depleted defences. It was the beginning of the end for the British, but Captain Baird didn't waver. He and his commanding officers managed once more to order their men into a square and, bereft of ammunition, made a valiant final stand, repulsing the Indians with only their swords and bayonets. Incredibly they managed to fight back 13 consecutive onslaughts. Eventually, the dwindling band of heroes could no longer face up to waves of thousands of fresh troops, many on horseback and elephants,who constantly came at them. Colonel Baillie surrendered and although they were promised fair treatment, the Indians immediately began murdering the survivors. Only the intervention of the French officers in Hyder Ali's camp prevented further bloodshed.

Colonel Baillie and Captian Baird were taken prisoner, along with 200 others who survived. Baird was seriously injured with wounds to his head, arm and leg. They were imprisoned in Seringapatam under horrendous conditions for three-and-a-half years. In 1784 hostilities ended temporarily and Captain Baird was released. But he was soon back in action. By now his regiment, the 73rd, had been renumbered to the 71st and renamed the Glasgow Highland Light Infantry, due to the huge numbers of rectruits from that city. In 1787 he was promoted to Major and three years later he was handed the rank of Lieutenant Colonel. He continued his rise through the ranks and in 1797 attained the rank of Brigadier General. A few months later he was a Major General.

The following year General Baird was back in Seringapatam, the scene of his unbearable incarceration. This time though he was there as an attacker. On May 4, 1799 Baird launched the attack and a few hours later it was under British control. As commanding officer of the victorious troops he assumed command of the town. The next day, however, he was ordered to hand control to Colonel Wellesley, who just happened to be the Governor General's brother. The colonel later made a name for himself as the Duke of Wellington.

The year 1802 saw him commanding the Egyptian Indain army which marched overland from Egypt to India. Three years later he was promoted to Lieutenant General and sent to sub- due the Dutch in the Cape of Good Hope on the southern tip of South Africa. He arrived on the 5th of the month and the job was completed 13 days later. His next major campaign was in 1809 when he lost his left arm at the Battle of Corunna in Spain. The British, with their Spanish and Portuguese allies, defeated Napoleon's army with Baird in command after the death of General Sir John Moore. As a reward Parliament honoured him with the Knight Grand Cross of the Bath and a Baronet. In 1810 Sir David married Miss Campbell-Preston of Perthshire. By now his fighting days were over but he was promoted again in 1814, this time to the rank of full general. It took six years before he was given another meaningfull task, as commander in chief of the forces in Ireland. His final military role was back in Scotland as commander of Fort George near Inverness. He died a year later leaving no children.

Another famous member of the Baird family was the Very Rev. Dr. George Husband Baird, who by the tender age of 33 had become the principal of Edinburgh University. He was born in 1761 and was a regular correspondent of Robert Burns and a subscriber to the first Kilmarnock edition of the poet's works. At university his interests lay in languages and he became fluent in many. He is chiefly remembered for his tireless work to improve religious education among the poorest children in the Highlands and Islands and in large towns. In his late 60s he was still able to travel extensively in the far north of the country promoting his ideals. He died in 1840 at his home in Linlithgow.

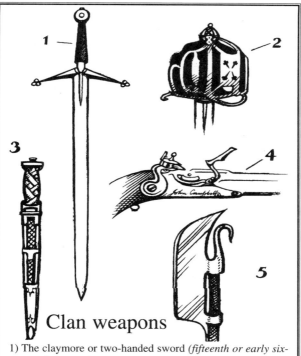

Clan weapons

1) The claymore or two-handed sword *(fifteenth or early six-teenth century)*
2) Basket hilt of broadsword made in Stirling, 1716
3) Highland dirk *(eighteenth century)*
4) Steel pistol *(detail)* made in Doune
5) Head of Lochaber Axe as carried in the '45 and earlier